BOOK SALE

COPY 5

J798.23
S Sholinsky, Jane
    In the saddle.

160	14
149	22
103	23
8	1
150	33
12	16
132	35
19	38

In the Saddle
HORSEBACK RIDING FOR GIRLS AND BOYS

BOOKS BY JANE SHOLINSKY

IN THE SADDLE: HORSEBACK RIDING FOR GIRLS AND BOYS

GROWING PLANTS FROM FRUITS AND VEGETABLES

THE CHALLENGE OF SKIING

In the Saddle

HORSEBACK RIDING FOR GIRLS AND BOYS

by Jane Sholinsky

Photographs by
Dan S. Nelken

Julian Messner New York

Published by Julian Messner, a Simon & Schuster Division of Gulf & Western Corporation. Simon & Schuster Building, 1230 Avenue of the Americas, New York, N.Y. 10020. All rights reserved.

Copyright © 1977 by Jane Sholinsky

Printed in the United States of America

Design by Ruth Bornschlegel

Second Printing, 1978

Library of Congress Cataloging in Publication Data
Sholinsky, Jane.

   In the saddle.
   SUMMARY: Discusses equipment, correct position for riding, the horse's gaits and how to "go" with them, safety tips, and horse show competition.
     1. Horsemanship—Juvenile literature.
[1. Horsemanship] I. Nelken, Dan S. II. Title.
SF309.2.S54   798'.23   76-52388
ISBN 0-671-32825-5

For Marc Adam

The author wishes to thank the following individuals who appear in the photographs in this book: Nancy Luden, Kathleen Gilrain, Elaine Carlsen, Ellen McCartin, Gina Tinker, Shellee Lounsbury, Dari Lain Kaplan, Dawn Detwiller, and John Montaldo, Jr.

Special thanks is also offered to Millicent Montaldo for her kind help.

Appreciation is expressed to Joanna Cohn, manager of Two Penny Farm, Katonah, New York, where the photographs were taken.

CONTENTS

1. Learning the Right Way · 9
2. Before You Begin · 11
3. Proper Equipment · 16
4. Getting Ready to Ride · 31
5. Learning to Ride · 48
6. On Your Own · 61
7. Horse Show Competition · 67

Glossary · 75

Index · 78

1. LEARNING THE RIGHT WAY

The young people in this photograph are part of a fast growing group of horse lovers. Like many other girls and boys throughout the country, they are learning to ride.

Horseback riding is not a difficult sport to learn. Anyone can be taught to ride. Naturally, the more often you ride, the better you will be at it. But you don't have to be an expert to enjoy the sport.

It isn't even necessary for you to own your own

horse. There are many stables and riding academies where you can ride one or two horses regularly. Many of these stables also offer lessons. And the best and safest way to learn to ride properly is by taking lessons.

Riding is not just a matter of climbing on a horse and galloping off into the sunset. Even if you have ridden before, you should take lessons. It is better to learn correctly the first time than have to break bad habits later on.

As you become a better rider, you will realize how important it is to treat your horse with understanding and kindness. Caring for the horse and never abusing the animal are as important as riding correctly—even more so.

2.
BEFORE YOU BEGIN

Every new rider should become familiar with the parts of a horse. This doesn't mean you must memorize every part of a horse's anatomy. But a general knowledge will make it easier for you to follow directions when learning to ride.

It is also helpful to know how to tell one horse from another. One way is by their coloring. A horse that is all brown or all black has no special name. But a brown horse with a black mane and tail is called a *bay*. Most *bay* horses also have black lower legs.

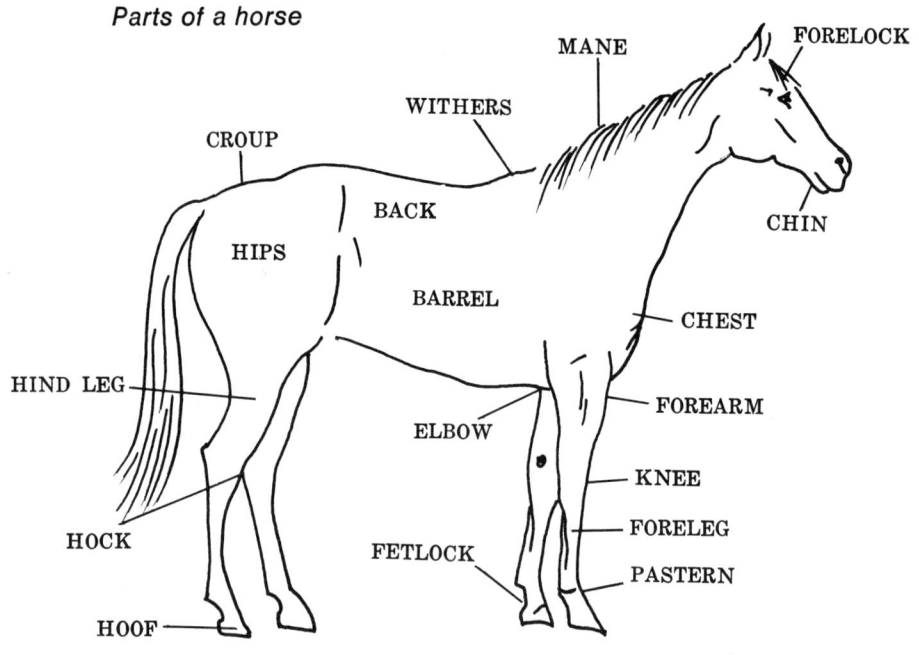

Parts of a horse

Horses that range in color from a light shade of red to a deep copper are *chestnuts*. In the West, they are sometimes called *sorrels*. Their mane and tail are usually the same color as their body hair. But they can also be a little lighter.

Roan is any solid color with a sprinkling of white hairs throughout. A roan may be a chestnut and white mixture (strawberry roan), a black and white mixture (blue roan), or a bay and white mixture (red roan).

Other two-tone horses are the *pinto* and the *Appaloosa*. Both of these horses, along with the *palomino*, a golden color horse with a white mane and tail, are the names of a breed as well as a color.

There are other ways to identify horses. You can also describe them by the special white markings they carry.

A wide white band running down the front of a horse's face is called a *blaze*. A white patch on the fore-

Horse with a blaze

14 • IN THE SADDLE

head is a *star*. A mark of white at or between the horse's nostrils is a *snip*. And a white leg is known as a *stocking*.

Another way to classify horses is by age. A *filly* is a female horse under the age of four. After her fourth birthday, she is a *mare*. A male horse is a *colt* until he is four. Then he becomes a *stallion*, unless he has been castrated. (This is a surgical process which eliminates the ability to have offspring.) In that case, he is a *gelding*.

You will find most riding horses in a stable are mares and geldings. They, like all horses, respond to gentleness and kindness.

Horse with stockings

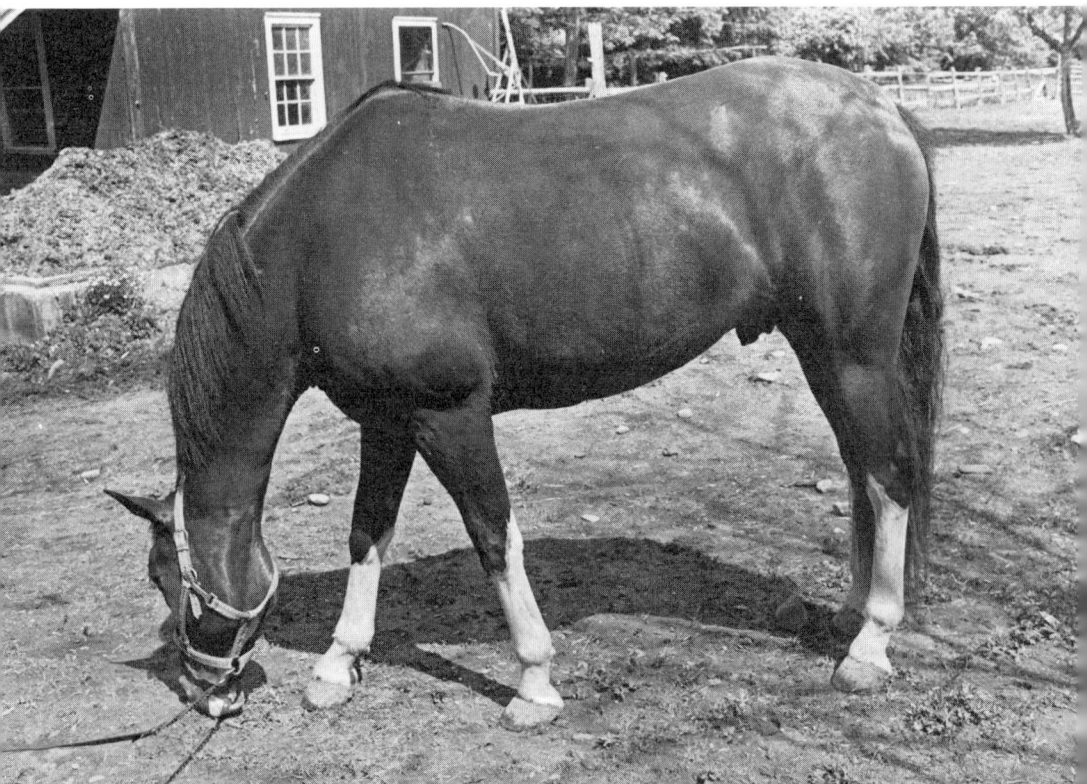

When getting to know the horse you are going to ride, it is fine to offer him an apple, carrot, or lump of sugar. Just hold the treat in the palm of your hand and hold your hand out flat.

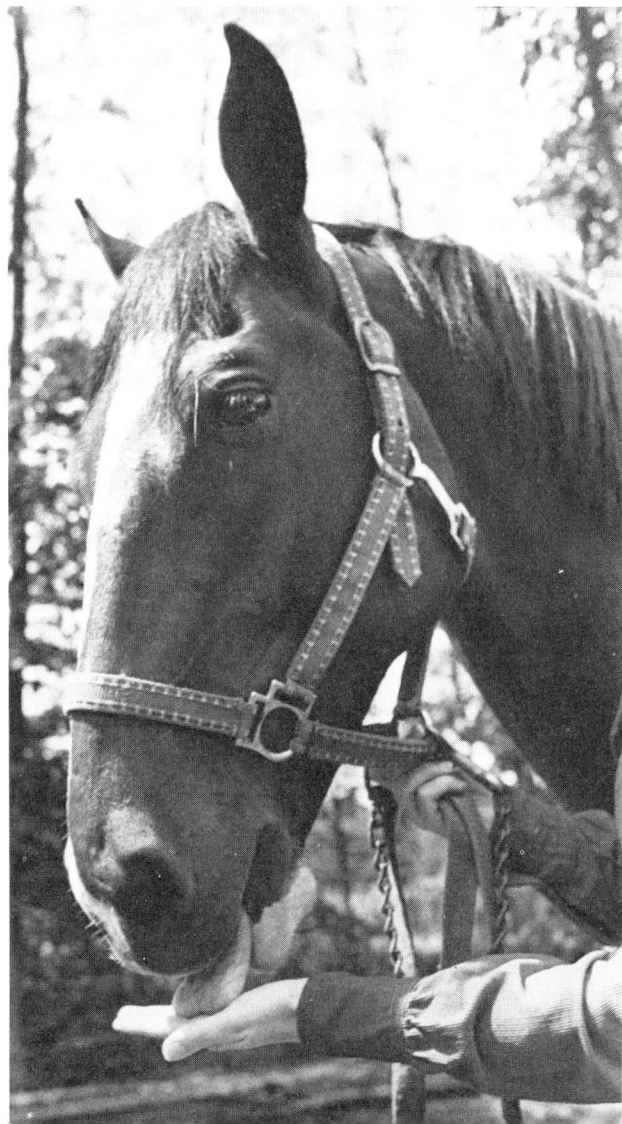

Proper way for a rider to offer a treat

3.

PROPER EQUIPMENT

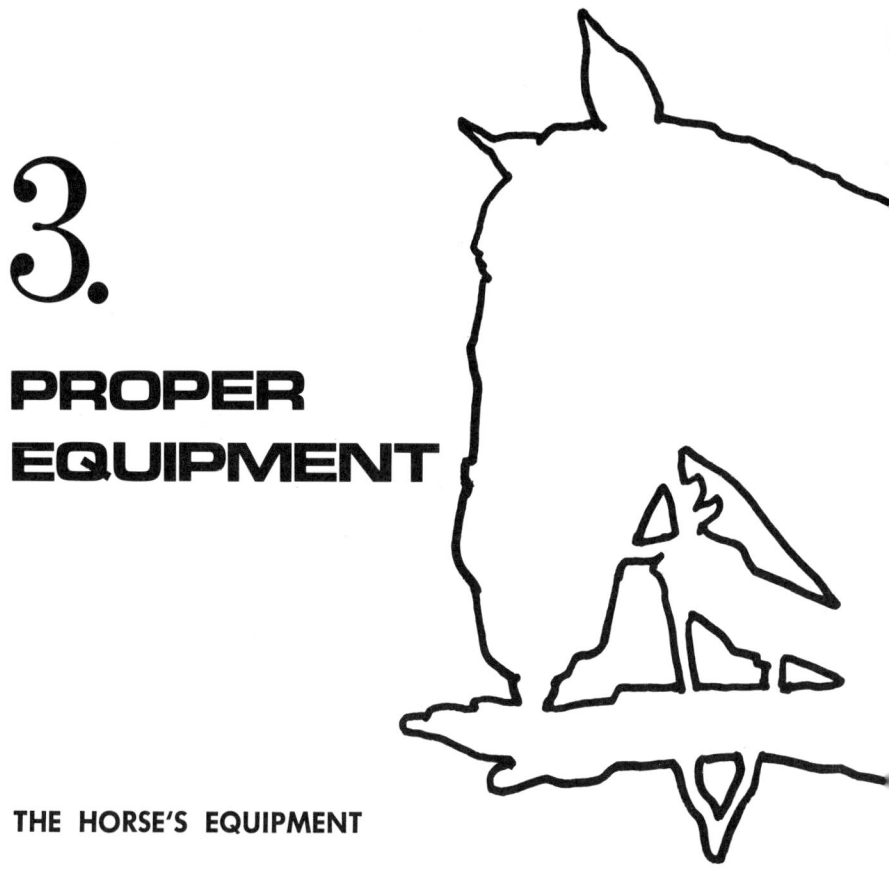

THE HORSE'S EQUIPMENT

The equipment used for horseback riding is called *tack*. It consists of two main pieces: the *saddle* and the *bridle*. The saddle goes on the horse's back. The bridle, which is used to control the horse, fits on the horse's head.

THE SADDLE

All saddles are made of wood and covered with several layers of leather. The front of a saddle is known as

Saddle and bridle in position

the *pommel*. The back part, which curves upward, is the *cantle*.

An English saddle, the type generally used at riding academies, is held onto the horse by a strap called a *girth*. On Western saddles, these straps are called *cinches*.

The girth is buckled onto straps called *billets*. Leather flaps beneath the billets keep the buckles from pinching the horse. Then outer flaps, called *skirts*, cover the billets to protect the rider's legs.

Stirrup leathers are attached to the saddle outside the skirts. Buckles on the leathers allow the *stirrups* to be adjusted shorter or longer.

18 • IN THE SADDLE

Under the saddle, a horse often wears a saddle pad to protect his back. These are usually made of heavy felt or sheepskin, and are the same size as the saddle.

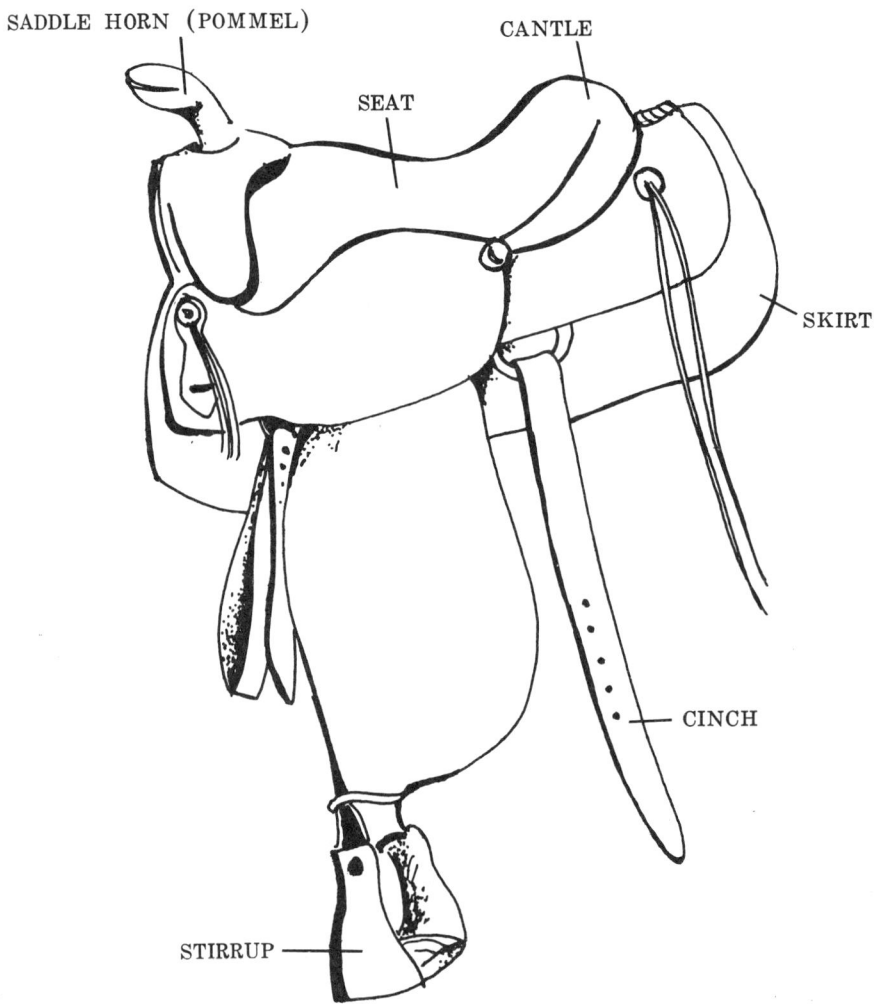

Western saddle

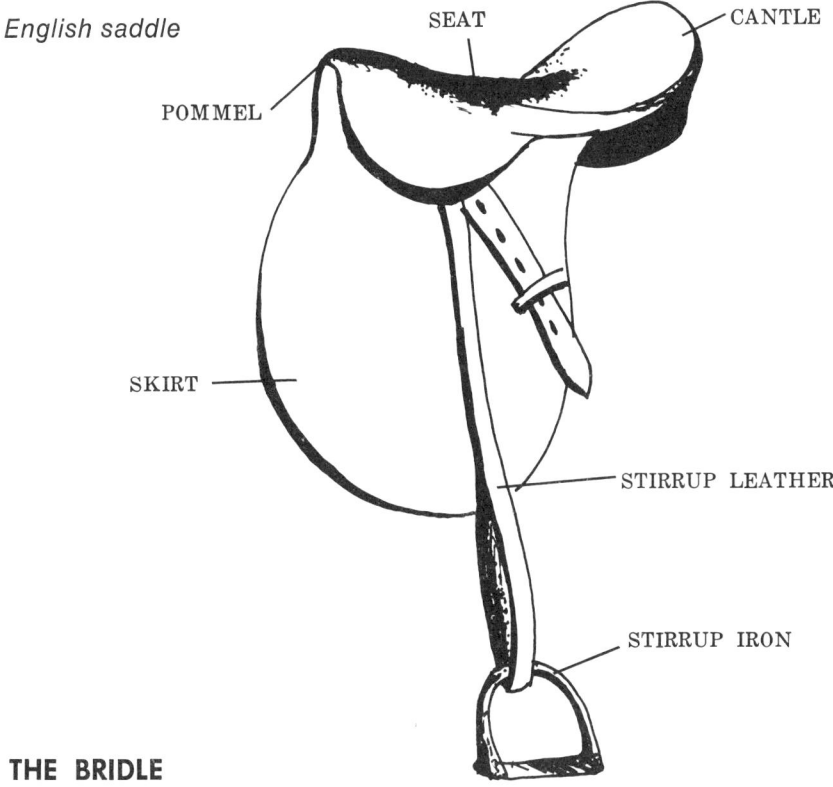

English saddle

THE BRIDLE

All bridles are basically the same. They consist of a crownpiece, a noseband, the bit and the reins. The only real difference between one bridle and another is the type of bit used.

A *bit* is a metal mouthpiece. It fits inside the horse's mouth between his front and back teeth. Together with the *reins*, it is used to guide the horse.

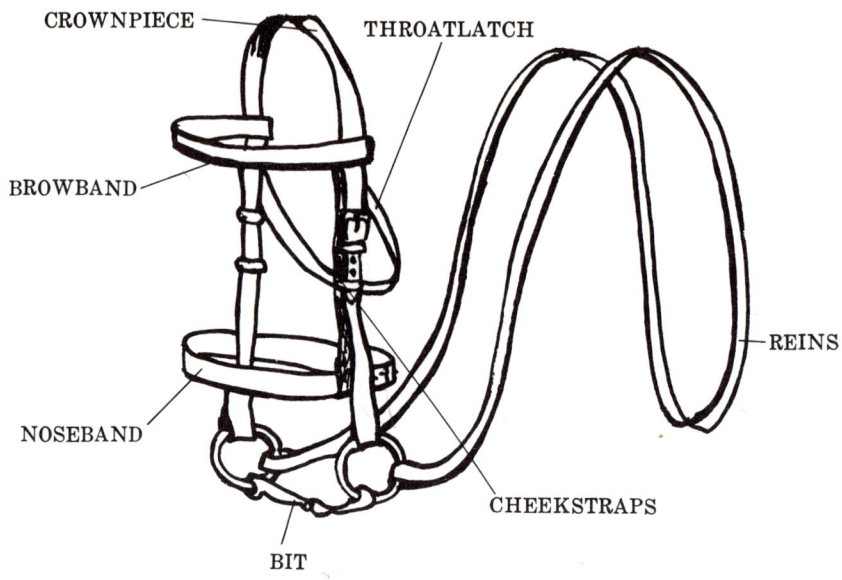

Parts of a bridle

There are many types of bits and bit combinations. Some put little pressure on the horse's mouth, and some put a great deal of pressure on it. The bit you use will depend on how well your hands work the reins, and on the horse you are riding.

The three basic types of bits are the snaffle, the pelham, and the curb. A *snaffle* bit is a bar which is jointed or hinged in the middle. It is considered a mild bit because it puts most of the pressure on the corners of the horse's mouth. A snaffle bit requires only one rein, but it can be used with double reins also.

If you are a beginning rider, your horse will probably have a snaffle bit. Both a beginning rider and a heavy-handed one tend to jerk and put unnecessary pressure on their horse's mouth.

Proper Equipment • 21

A *pelham* bit is a little more severe than the snaffle. It has a straight bar that fits inside the horse's mouth. Then a *curb chain*, or strap, fastens under the horse's chin. The pelham bit requires two sets of reins. When a rider pulls on the reins, the horse feels pressure against the back of his mouth as well as the back of his chin.

The *curb* bit is usually used on a horse that is difficult to handle. It is a steel bar with a sharp curve in the middle. The curb bit also has a chain which fastens under the horse's chin. When a rider pulls on the reins, the bit presses on the roof of the horse's mouth and the curb strap presses against the horse's chin.

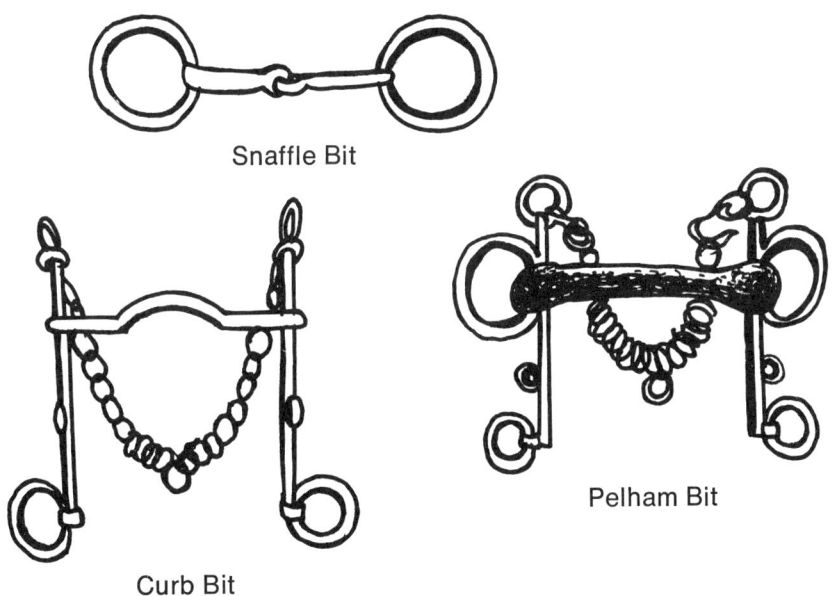

Three types of bits

22 • IN THE SADDLE

Often the curb and snaffle bits are used together. This combination is called a *full, or double, bridle*. It is used with two sets of reins, one for each bit. The *snaffle rein* is always on top, and can be used separately or together with the *curb rein*.

Some horses also wear a *martingale* in addition to the saddle and the bridle. This is a long strap that goes from the noseband on the bridle to the girth of the saddle. The reason for using a martingale is to hold down the horse's head. This keeps a horse from carrying or throwing his head too high and getting out of control.

Wearing a martingale

TACKING UP

As a beginning rider, your horse will probably be "tacked up"—saddled and bridled—and led out each time you ride. However, the time may come when you will have to tack up your own mount.

The most important thing to learn is that most horses are trained to be handled from their left, or *near*, side. Therefore, always work from the left side of your horse.

Never, never go around the horse's rear, if you don't have to. Horses are easily startled. When frightened, a horse will instinctively kick out with his hind legs. In the open, keep a good distance away from his hooves. In the stall, if you must cross behind your horse, do exactly the opposite: keep in close. If he feels nervous, all he will do is shove you with his hind quarters, since he can't get his heels up for a good kick.

Before you saddle your horse, be sure the *stirrups* are at the top of their *leathers*, and the girth is over the seat of the saddle. Then place the saddle high on the horse's *withers*, and let it slide back between his shoulder blades. This will smooth the hair on the horse's back and help prevent saddle sores.

Once the saddle is in place, let the girth down on the

Lifting saddle onto horse's back

right side. Then check to be sure it is not twisted before you fasten it to the *billet* straps.

Tighten the girth until it is snug. Wait a few moments, and check it again. Horses often blow up their stomachs when they are being saddled. If you wait until they relax and their stomachs go down, you can readjust the girth. To fit properly, you should be able to slip two fingers between the horse's ribs and the girth.

To bridle your horse, first slip the reins over the horse's neck. Then hold the bit in your left hand and the crownpiece in your right. Now, lift up the bridle so the horse's nose slips into the noseband. With your left hand, carefully guide the bit into the horse's mouth.

Fastening the girth to the billet straps

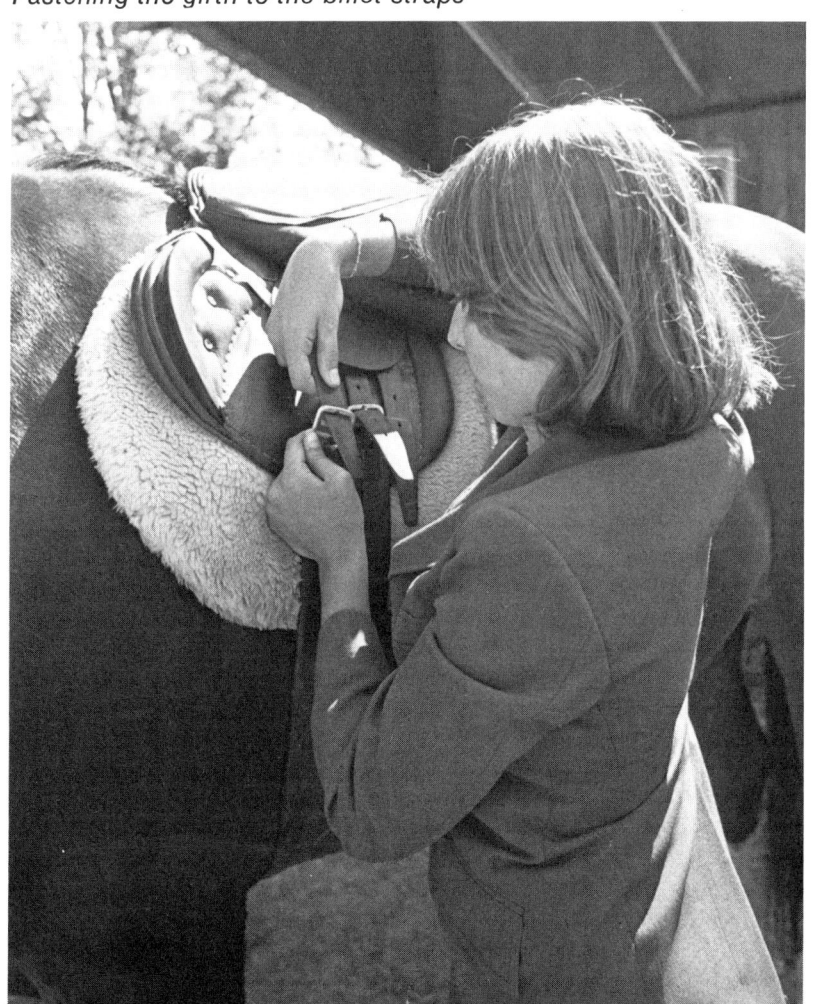

26 • IN THE SADDLE

A horse will usually open his mouth when a bit is placed against his teeth. If your horse doesn't, place your thumb and index finger into the space between his front and back teeth. This will make him open up.

Putting the bridle on the horse

Fastening the throatlatch

Once the bit is in place, fix the crownpiece up over the horse's ears. Then fasten the *throatlatch*. If there is a curb chain, be sure it is smooth before securing it. Last, but certainly not least, check the curb chain and throatlatch. Be sure each is loose enough to fit two fingers between it and the horse's jaw.

THE RIDER'S EQUIPMENT

Now that your horse has been outfitted, what will you need to ride?

Until you're sure horseback riding is for you, a pair of jeans, and sturdy leather shoes with low heels will do nicely.

Two clothing *don't's* when riding horseback:

DON'T ride in shorts or a bathing suit unless you are riding bareback. Otherwise your legs and thighs will be rubbed raw by the saddle flaps and stirrup leathers.

DON'T ever wear sneakers or sandals when riding with a saddle. Your feet may slip through the stirrup irons and trap you in a dangerous position.

If you do buy a riding outfit, make sure your clothes are well-fitting. For casual riding, boots, jodhpur pants, breeches, or chaps and a riding shirt or sweater are fine.

English riding boots come in two lengths—ankle-high and knee-high. Ankle-high boots are called jodhpur boots. They are worn with jodhpur pants which come down to cover the ankle.

Knee-high boots, sometimes called hunt boots, are worn with breeches. This style of riding pants is often flared slightly at the thigh and end just below the knee. When buying hunt boots, be sure they are the right length. They should come up to right below your knee. It is also important that they fit properly in the foot

Rider on left wears hunt boots and breeches; on right, rider wears jodhpurs and boots

and along the calf of the leg. A boot that is too wide will allow your leg to swim around inside. This will cut down on your leg grip.

The style of your jacket will depend on the rest of your outfit. The jacket usually worn with hunt boots and breeches is shorter than the one worn with jodhpurs. It is also not as close-fitted.

To finish off your outfit, you will need a hard hat or derby. Not all riders feel comfortable wearing a hat. However, a hard hunt cap is a must for head protection

30 • IN THE SADDLE

when jumping. A rider who doesn't wear one is very foolish.

If you ride Western-style, cowboy boots and jeans are the standard outfit. A jacket and wide-brimmed cowboy hat may also be worn.

Western style outfit

4.
GETTING READY TO RIDE

The first step is learning how to approach and lead a horse. When you approach a horse, step up alongside his left shoulder. Walk up slowly. Don't rush or grab at him. Horses are jumpy animals. Their big eyes can see in a full circle (much more than we can). Any sudden movement can startle them.

To lead a horse, take the reins in your right hand just below the bit. The reins may be either looped over the horse's withers, or pulled forward over the horse's

Leading horse

head, with the end of the rein held in your left hand. Pulled forward is the preferred method, especially if you are not going to mount right away.

Getting Ready to Ride • 33

When you are ready to walk, face forward and step out slowly. Look straight ahead as you walk, not at the horse. As long as you have a firm grip on the reins, the horse will walk beside you quietly.

HOW TO MOUNT

You always mount a horse from the left. This is a habit that has come down to us from the days of chivalry in France and England. A knight swung himself into the saddle from the left side of the horse to keep his right arm (the arm in which he held his sword) free.

Before you mount, be sure to check the girth. If you can slip more than two fingers between the horse's ribs and the girth, it needs to be tightened another notch or two.

To mount from the ground, stand so you are facing toward the horse's rear. Gather the reins in your left hand, and place your hand on the horse's withers. If the horse has a mane, you can grab onto it instead.

While your left hand is on the horse's withers, use your right hand to turn the stirrup toward you. Then place the ball of your left foot on the stirrup *iron*.

Now grab hold of the *cantle* with your right hand, and count to three. Then spring up into a standing position. A good spring should let you stand up straight in

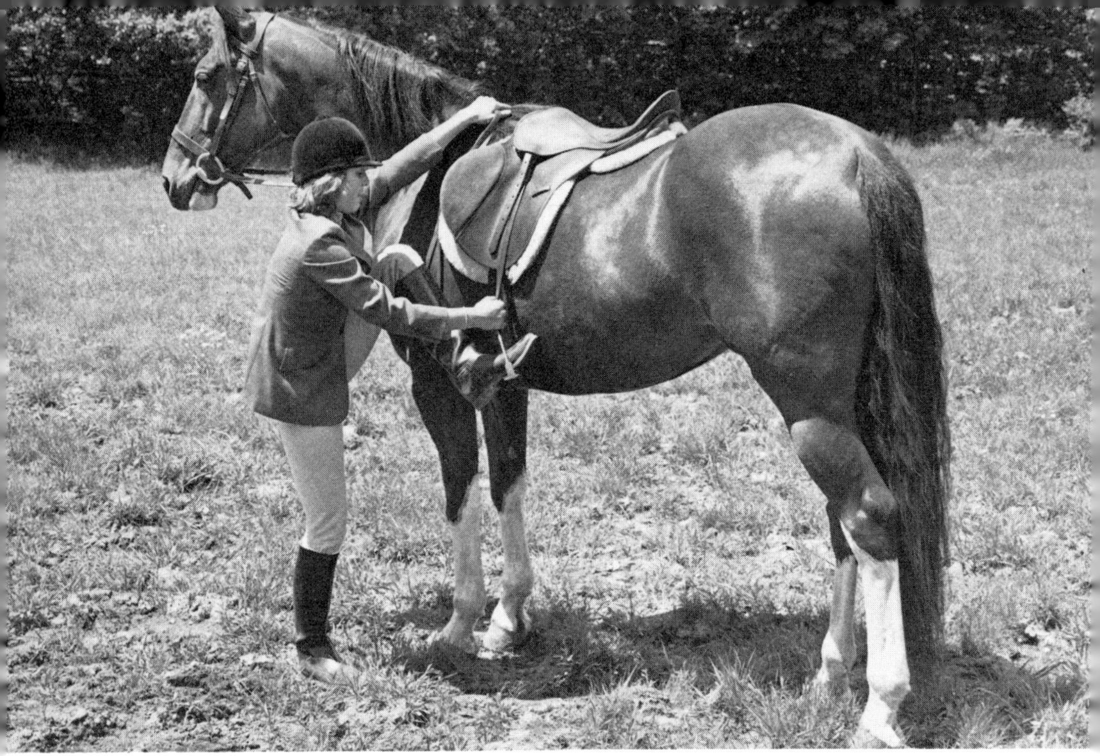

Getting Ready to Ride • 35

the stirrup. However, if you are small, like the rider in the photograph, you might have to use your arms to help pull as you spring off the ground.

Once you are in a standing position, grab the *pommel* with your right hand, and swing your right leg high over the saddle. Be sure to swing your leg high enough so it clears the horse's back.

Opposite page, top: *In mounting position, holding stirrup for left foot*
Opposite page, bottom: *Springing into standing position*
Below: *Swinging leg over saddle*

36 • IN THE SADDLE

Now gently let yourself down into the saddle, and place your right foot in the stirrup. Never drop down into the saddle. A sudden jolt like that could startle your horse, and he might jump forward before you are properly set.

As you practice these moves a few times, you will be surprised at how easy mounting a horse really is.

Some riders may need the help of a *mounting block*. If this applies to you, follow the same procedure as

In completed mounting position

Using a mounting block

mounting from the ground. Only, face the horse when placing your left foot in the stirrup.

POSITION IN THE SADDLE

Your position in the saddle is usually called your *seat*. A balanced seat is the key to good horsemanship. When you are balanced in the saddle, you will not have to cling to the reins or saddle for support.

38 • IN THE SADDLE

For a balanced seat, sit in the middle of the saddle, but do not rest on your buttocks as if you were seated in a chair. Instead, shove your buttocks to the rear of the saddle, and rest on your thighs.

Keep your thighs, knees, and calves in close contact with the horse. Then place both feet in the stirrups and push your heels well down. This position will force your weight into your heels where it should be. It may feel a little awkward at first, but soon you will do it without giving it a thought.

To maintain a balanced seat, your upper body should be straight but not stiff. It is also important to keep

Position of seat and legs in the saddle

Position of upper body and hands in the saddle

your elbows close to your sides, and your hands over the horse's withers about two inches apart.

It takes time and practice to learn the correct position. To check if you have a balanced seat, try to stand in the stirrups without holding onto the reins or saddle. If you cannot stand up easily, you are not properly

Standing in stirrups

balanced. Tell yourself: chin up, back straight, buttocks to the rear, and heels down. Then try it again. And again. And again. . . .

ADJUSTING STIRRUPS

After you assume a balanced seat, if something still feels awkward, chances are it's your stirrups. As a rule, when stirrups are the correct length, the tread (flat bottom)

Checking for correct length of stirrups

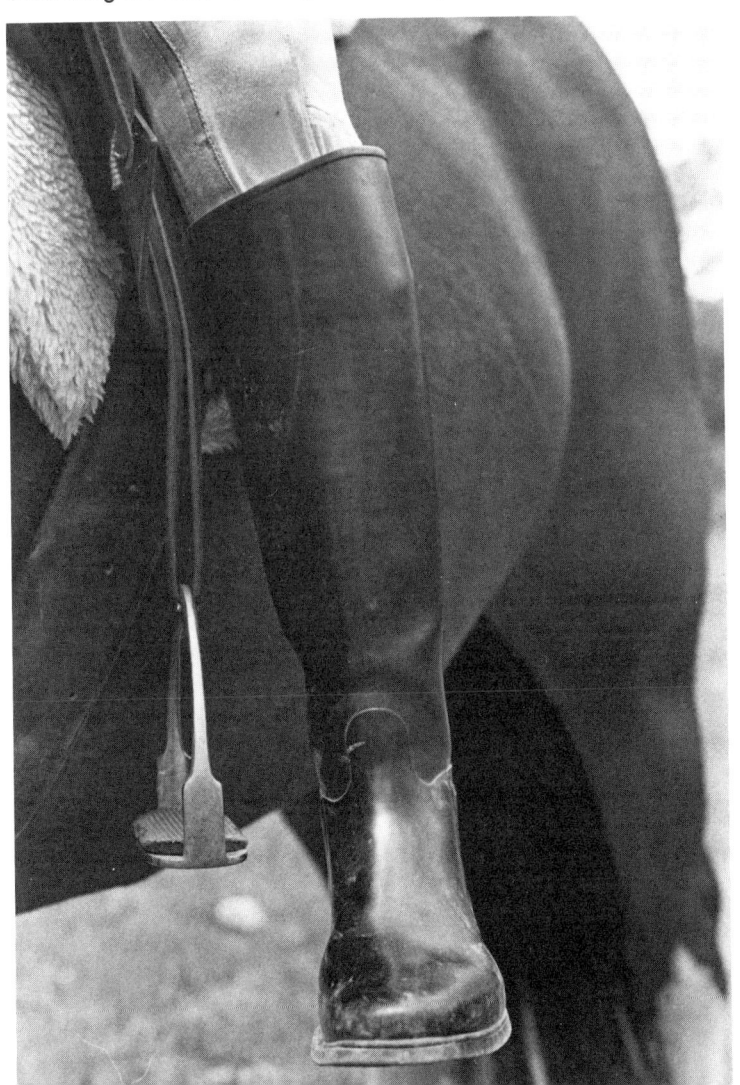

is level with your ankle bone when your leg hangs straight down. However, some riders are more comfortable with either a slightly shorter or longer length stirrup.

When adjusting your stirrup length, remember your boots must be able to make contact with the horse's flanks. A rider whose stirrups are too short is pushed back in the saddle, and cannot make contact in the right places. A rider whose stirrups are too long will find it difficult controlling legs as well as balance.

Once your stirrups are adjusted, rest the ball of each foot on the stirrup treads. Then slide each foot next to the inner side of the stirrup irons, and bend your ankles in toward the horse.

HOLDING THE REINS

Next to balance, your hands and the reins are two of the most important aids to becoming a good rider. They are the direct line of communication between you and your horse.

When riding English-style, you should hold the reins in both hands. Some riders prefer to grasp each rein in a fist, while others prefer to hold the reins in a three-finger grip. Either way is acceptable, as long as you

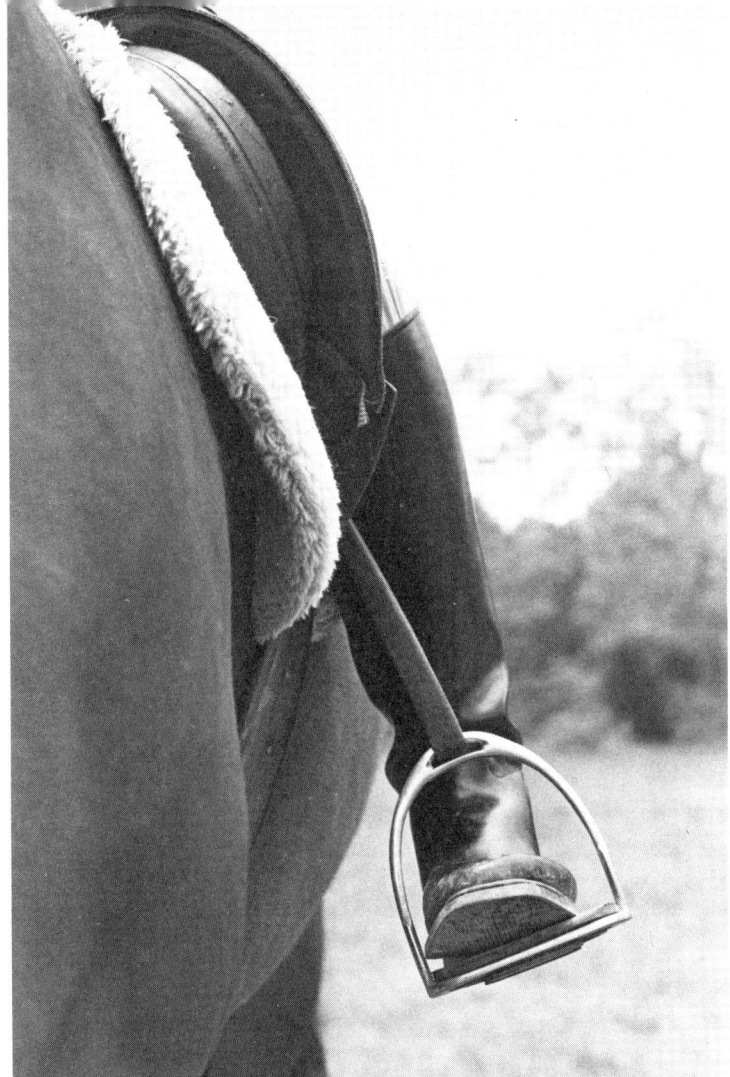
Rider's foot on inner side of iron

hold your hands so the reins form a straight line from your elbow to the horse's mouth.

To hold a single rein, or snaffle, in a three-finger grip, place the rein between your little finger and your ring finger. Then run the rein through the palm of your hand and up between your thumb and forefinger. Hold each rein firmly to prevent it from slipping. Then place the *bight* (ends of the rein) on the right side of the horse's neck.

The three-finger grip for a double rein is much the same as for one rein. To hold a double rein, loop the snaffle (top rein) around your little finger. Then place the curb (lower rein) between your ring finger and your little finger. Bring both reins up through the palm of your hand, and grip them between your thumb and forefinger. Be sure you have a good grip on the reins, then check to see that the snaffle is on the outside.

Holding single rein

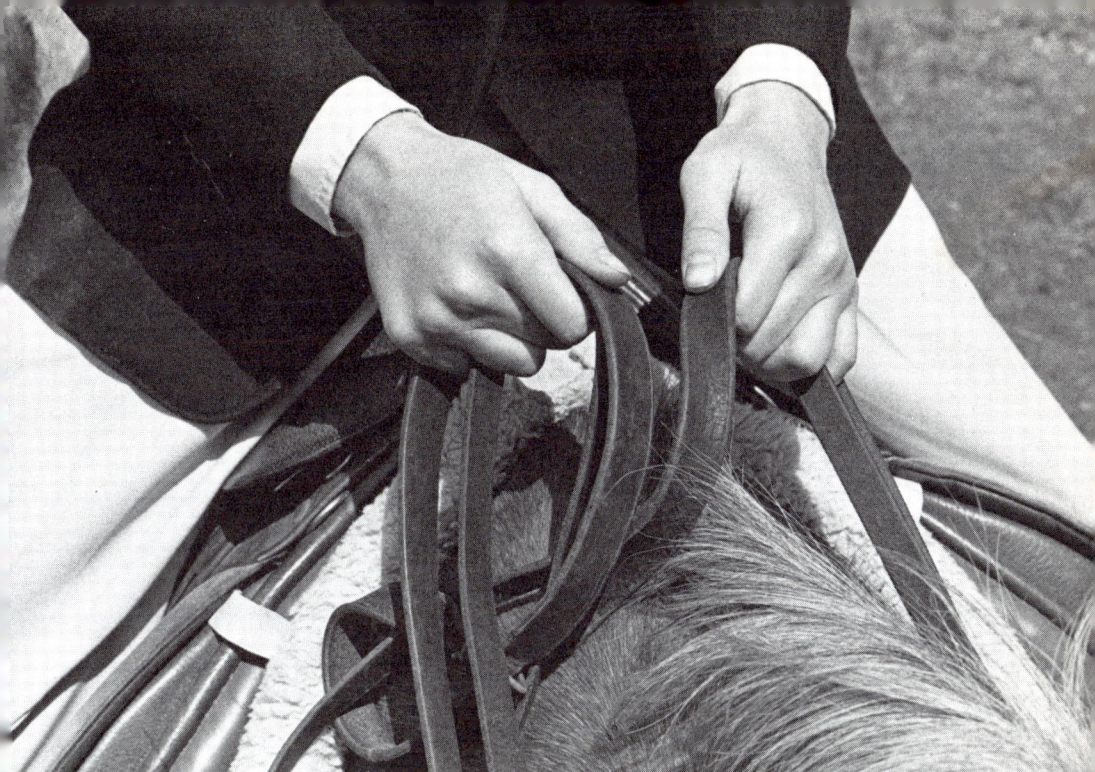

Holding double rein

The proper way to hold your reins, when riding Western-style, is to hold them in one hand. Both reins are held in your left hand between your thumb and forefinger. Keep your left hand just over the pommel, and hold your thumb pointing forward.

DISMOUNTING

Getting off the horse is almost the exact opposite of getting on. To dismount, gather the reins in your left hand,

Holding Western rein

and place the hand on the horse's withers. Remove your right foot from the stirrup, and swing your leg over the horse's back.

Prepare to slide off the horse by shifting your right hand to the cantle. Then, leaning on both arms, remove your left foot from the stirrup. Now, slowly slide down off the horse, keeping both feet together.

One word of caution. Be sure to have both feet clear of the stirrups before sliding down. This way, should the horse decide to move, you won't get hung-up with a foot caught in the stirrup.

Dismounting

5.
LEARNING TO RIDE

When you take your first lesson, your instructor will tell you about your riding aids. They are your voice, your seat, your hands, and your legs—all the ways you communicate with your horse. Learning how to use these aids properly is important. They help you control your horse no matter what gait he is performing.

The horse has three natural *gaits*—the walk, the trot, and the gallop. The canter is not a separate gait, but a "collected," or slow gallop.

THE WALK

The *walk* is the slowest gait. A horse lifts his legs separately, one after the other. To signal your horse to walk, take up the slack in the reins so you have a light contact with the horse's mouth. Then lean forward slightly, and squeeze the horse with both your heels, just behind the girth.

Once the horse begins to walk, relax your hands and arms. Let them move with the motion of the horse's head. Be sure to look where you are going and not down

Walking position

at the horse. When you keep your head up, you will be balanced in the saddle so that nothing the horse can do will surprise you. If you keep your weight well down into your heels, your lower legs will be close to the horse's side. This lets you "talk" to your horse and give him directions without kicking him.

TURNING

In order to turn your horse, you must use a combination of your aids. When you want to turn right, look to the right. This slight change of position will shift your weight in the saddle. Then pull back lightly on the right rein. Never jerk on the rein or yank your horse's head around.

At the same time, use your legs to control the horse's hindquarters. As you pull on the right rein, apply pressure with the heel of your right leg. This helps to guide the horse into the turn, because a horse will move his hindquarters *away* from your leg pressure.

If you are riding Western-style and neckreining, you must shift the hand holding the reins in the direction of your turn. This presses the reins against the horse's neck. He will then move away from the pressure of the reins. To turn right, shift your hand to the right.

Turning horse

At the same time, apply pressure with your right leg.

Practice turning in both directions, keeping your horse at a walk. Remember to use your aids together—seat, hands, and legs.

Neckreining

STOPPING AND BACKING

To stop your horse, tighten your hands on the reins. Then sit deep in the saddle, and gently pull back on both reins

Learning to Ride • 53

by bending your wrists upward. If this doesn't bring the horse to a halt, shorten your reins. This will create more pressure on the bit as you pull back.

Once your horse has halted, try backing him up. To do this, squeeze your legs against the horse so he knows

Backing horse

54 • IN THE SADDLE

you want him to move. Then follow with the same procedure you did to stop him. After he takes a few steps backward, ease off on the pressure from your hands and legs. He will then come to a stop.

THE TROT

When you are secure in your seat at the walking gait, and are able to turn, stop and back up, you are ready for the next gait—the *trot*. A horse trots by moving diagonal legs. That is, the right foreleg moves with the left hind leg, and the left foreleg moves with the right hind leg.

On right diagonal

Riders refer to this as a right or left diagonal, depending on which front leg the horse has forward.

To signal your horse to go from a walk to a slow trot, take up any slack in your reins. This will alert the horse to the fact that something is about to happen. He will be waiting for the next command. Then squeeze the horse with both heels just behind the girth.

A horse trots with a one-two beat as each pair of diagonal legs hits the ground. To avoid being bounced, sit deep in the saddle and tighten your grip. Then lean slightly forward, letting your knees and ankles act as shock absorbers.

POSTING THE TROT

The faster a horse trots, the more difficult it is to sit in the saddle. Therefore, when you apply more leg pressure and move your horse into a fast trot, you should begin *posting*.

To post, you rise and sit in rhythm with the one-two beat. Always rise from the knees, not from the stirrups. Let the thrust of the horse help you out of the saddle. Don't try to pull yourself up.

Stay at the peak of the post just long enough to miss

a stride, then sit again. When you come down into the saddle, take care not to land heavily.

Once you feel comfortable posting, you are ready to pay attention to which *diagonal* you are posting on. When posting on the right diagonal, you will rise in the saddle as the horse's right leg moves forward, and sit when it hits the ground. To post on the left diagonal, follow the left leg in the same manner. Rise as the left leg moves forward, and sit as it hits the ground.

If you are trotting in a ring, you should post on the outside diagonal—the one next to the rail. At first, you

Posting on left diagonal

Posting to diagonal in ring

may have to glance down at the horse's shoulder to see which foreleg is moving forward. Later, however, you should be able to tell without looking.

Practice your posting on both the left and right diagonals. When you are trotting for a long distance, it is wise to change diagonals occasionally so as not to tire the horse. To change a diagonal, simply sit for one stride then resume posting.

THE CANTER

Once you have learned to rise from the saddle when posting the trot, it's time to learn to stay in the saddle at the *canter*.

When a horse canters, he moves in a three-beat gait. If the right foreleg appears to be *leading* (reaching out farther in the front than the other foreleg), the horse is said to be on a right lead. A horse cantering on the right lead: (1) starts out on the left hind leg; (2) then rolls onto the left front and right rear leg; (3) and ends on

Right lead canter

the right front leg. When cantering on a left lead: (1) the horse starts on the right hind leg; (2) then rolls onto the right front and left rear leg; (3) and winds up on the left front leg.

When cantering in a ring, it is important that the horse lead with his inside leg. If circling to the left, the horse should be on a left lead; to the right, on a right lead. This way the horse will always be leading with the inside leg. As he throws his weight into the turn, his inside legs will support both him and you.

SITTING THE CANTER

To signal your horse to a left-lead canter, turn the horse's head slightly to the right. Then sit forward in the saddle, and follow immediately with a squeeze of the right heel. In order to move away from your leg pressure, the horse will throw his weight onto his left side and step out with his left foreleg.

To put your horse on a right-lead canter, turn his head to the left, and squeeze with your left heel.

As soon as your horse is on the correct lead, straighten him out on the track.

Once your horse is in the canter—relax. This is the

Left lead canter

key to sitting the canter. Push your weight down into your heels. Then let your body rock in rhythm with the horse's movements.

At first, you will probably pound the saddle. But don't give up! Once you adjust to the horse's rhythm, you will be able to stay in close contact with the saddle.

6.
ON YOUR OWN

After you learn to ride, you are on your own. Good manners are important when riding. They are safety measures. Whether you ride in a ring, on the trail, or in an open field, a good rider avoids doing anything that may disturb other riders or frighten their horses.

One rule of good horsemanship is never to pass without warning. If you must pass, always do so on the right, and don't come tearing up from behind. Slow down a little. Call out "passing," or "on your right" to let the other rider know you are coming—and then make your move.

Another rule is that riders walking their horses in a ring should stay on the inside of the *track*. That is, close to the center of the ring. This leaves room for those riders moving at a faster gait to pass on the outside.

On the trail, ride in pairs whenever the trail is wide enough. Let the better rider keep closest to any oncoming horses.

Never follow the horse in front of you too closely. He may kick out at your horse and frighten his rider.

Rider passing on the outside of the track in a ring

On the trail, following at a horse's length apart

On the other hand, when riding in a group, especially on the trail, don't get too far behind. This is not fair to the other riders who will have to wait up for you.

If your horse balks when passing some object like a fallen tree, let another horse and rider go first. Then squeeze your legs against the horse's side to urge him ahead. If your horse still refuses, ask another mounted rider to lead your horse past the object by holding the cheekstraps of your horse's bridle.

Never keep your horse at the same gait for a long period of time. Also, don't ever let him become overheated.

If at any time you have to stop your horse, pull over to the side of the trail. Or move to the center of the ring.

Rider has stopped horse in center of the ring

Don't *ever* stop in the track. Another rider moving at a fast gait may not see you in time to stop. This could result in a serious accident.

Speaking of accidents, at one time or another every rider takes a spill. It is not as frightening as it may seem. The trick is to know how to fall. If you fall properly, chances are you will not get hurt seriously.

When you feel yourself falling, don't fight it. Relax and let yourself go. As long as you don't tense up, the most damage will probably be a black and blue mark or two.

Once you fall off, get right back on. A horse can sense if you are frightened. So don't give yourself time to think of what just happened. Get right back on, and continue your ride. Before you know it, you'll be able to laugh about your spill.

If your horse rears, don't panic. Grab onto his mane to avoid tugging on the reins, and move all your weight as far forward as you can. As the horse goes down, pull his head down with one rein and kick him with the opposite leg. This should force him to go in a circle, and he cannot rear. Keep him moving. A horse can rear only from a standing position.

If your horse requires the use of a *crop* (also called a bat, whip, or stick), be sure you use it properly. A crop

Carrying crop

should be carried in your hand along with the reins. To warn the horse, slap the crop against his shoulder. A slight flick of the wrist is all you need.

Never wave a crop or use it any other way. Remember, horses are jumpy animals. Another horse seeing the crop may become frightened, and a frightened horse can get the best rider into trouble.

Always walk your horse for the last 10 or 15 minutes of the ride. This lets him cool off. In warm weather, you may have to dismount and walk the horse on foot. In that case, walk in the center of the ring. Be sure the horse is cool *and* dry before you send him back to the stall.

Walking horse at end of ride

7.
HORSE SHOW COMPETITION

There is a certain excitement in horse show competition. All eyes are on you, especially the judge's. Everyone is watching you and judging your performance.

Once you become a good rider, you may want to enter into competition. The perfect place to begin is a local horse show. It will give you the experience you need. From there, if you are serious about becoming a champion rider, you can begin working your way up to the big-time show circuit.

68 • IN THE SADDLE

Most local horse show classes fall into two groups: Horsemanship, in which the rider is judged, and classes for the horse. In horsemanship classes, you are judged on how well you maintain good riding form while making your horse respond to various commands.

The classes where the horse is judged vary. In some classes, a horse is judged for his ability to jump. In others, for his beauty or his good manners in the ring.

Before you enter a show, ask for a prize list. It will give all the information about the show: the types of classes in the show, entry requirements for each class, and the entry fee. Make note of the classes you are

Taking horse over jump in horse show

qualified for. Then enter the ones in which you will do best.

When you enter a horse show, you receive a show number. This is your identification. Hook it onto the

Wearing horse show number

70 · IN THE SADDLE

back of your jacket collar so it can be seen. This way, everyone, especially the judge, will know who you are.

When the show begins, listen carefully to the announcements of classes over the loud speaker. In classes where you perform over fences, you will be called into the ring one at a time. In classes on the flat (no fences), however, all contestants enter the ring together.

Once you are in the ring, proceed at a walk along the rail. When all contestants are in the ring, the ringmaster will call out commands to walk, trot, canter, and reverse.

Try to obey these commands as quickly as possible.

Entering show ring

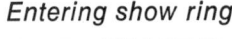

If at any time your horse breaks his gait, or takes the wrong lead, slow him up. Then begin again immediately. Also, don't let yourself get bunched in with the other riders. If you feel yourself getting caught in a jam, cut through the center of the ring. This will get you away from the crowd. When the competition is over, you will be asked to line up in the center of the ring. Always line up facing the ringmaster. This way, the judge can stand behind you and the other riders to see the numbers.

Occasionally, the judge may feel two or more riders had equally good rounds. In this case, the judge will ask them to perform additional paces, usually in a figure

Lined up after competition

eight. By asking a rider to make a figure eight at the trot, the judge can tell if the rider knows the proper diagonals and how to change them. At the canter, a figure eight tests the rider's ability to make the horse change leads.

If you are asked to perform a figure eight, move to the center of the ring. Then make two big circles, one to the left and one to the right. It does not matter if you start to the right or left, but your circles *must* meet in the center of the ring.

As you complete the first circle, slow your horse to a walk for one or two strides. Then go on to make the next circle to complete your figure eight. Each time you finish a figure eight, bring your horse to a full stop in the center of the ring. At the end of your last figure eight, stop your horse and back up a few steps.

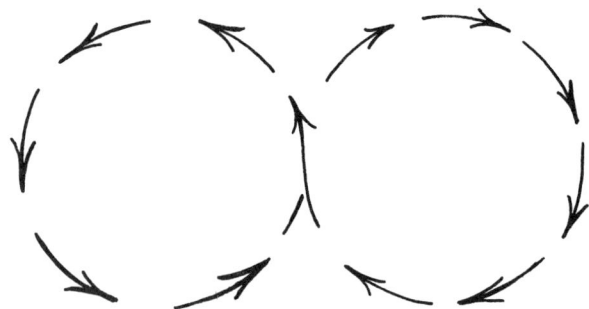

Pattern of a figure eight

Horse Show Competition · 73

After you have completed these paces, return to your place in line. Then wait for the winners to be announced. If your number is called, ride forward to accept your prize.

Accepting ribbon at horse show

74 • IN THE SADDLE

In horsemanship classes, the prizes usually consist of six ribbons. A blue ribbon is presented for first place. Then red, yellow, white, pink, and green, in that order.

If you are a winner, thank the person presenting you with your ribbon. If you have lost, take the loss without hard feelings. Good sportsmanship is also important in horse show competition. It is part of what makes a horse show fun.

Showing good sportsmanship at end of a horse show

GLOSSARY

AGE: Horses are fully mature at 7 years of age and often live to beyond 30. An aged horse is one of 9 years or more.

AIDS: The signals given to a horse to make him perform in a certain way. They may be given by the rider's voice, legs, hands, or seat.

APPALOOSA: A breed of horse with mixed colors, characterized by a spotted rump.

BAY: A color ranging from sandy to reddish brown or dark brown. A bay colored horse has a black mane and tail and very often black stockings.

BIGHT: The ends of the reins.

BILLETS: Saddle straps to which the girth is attached.

BIT: The part of the bridle the horse holds in his mouth.

BLAZE: A wide white band that runs down the front of a horse's face.

BRIDLE: The leather head harness which supports the bit in the horse's mouth and, together with the reins, is used to guide the horse.

CANTER: A three-beat gait which is an easy gallop.

CANTLE: The raised hind part of a saddle.

CHESTNUT: A reddish coat color ranging from light red to deep copper. The mane and tail of a chestnut horse are of the same or slightly lighter color.

CINCHES: Double girths attached to a western saddle.

COLT: A male horse up to the age of 4.

CROP: An aid in riding. Also called a bat, stick, or whip.

CURB: A steel bar bit with a sharp curve in the middle. It also has a chain, or strap that fastens under the horse's chin.

GLOSSARY

CURB CHAIN: A strap or chain attached to the bit.

EQUESTRIAN: A person who rides horses.

FILLY: A female horse up to the age of 4.

FOAL: A new-born horse of either sex.

GAIT: Any of the ways a horse moves—a walk, trot, canter, gallop, etc.

GALLOP: The horse's fastest gait.

GELDING: A castrated male horse.

GIRTH: The band that goes underneath the horse to hold the saddle in place.

IRONS: The metal parts of the stirrups.

MARE: A female horse over the age of four.

MARTINGALE: A strap passing between the forelegs of a horse connecting the girth with the bit. It is used on some horses to keep their heads down.

NEAR SIDE: The left side of a horse. The right side of a horse is referred to as the "off" side.

PALOMINO: Describes both a color and a breed of horse. Originally used to describe a golden color horse with a white mane and tail. The palomino, the Appaloosa, and the pinto are the only cases in the horse world where a particular color may be registered as a breed.

PELHAM: A single-bar bit that features a curb chain which fastens under the horse's chin and to which a second set of reins are attached.

PINTO: A horse with a spotted coat.

POMMEL: The front part of the saddle that curves upward.

Glossary • 77

POSTING: The act of alternately rising from the saddle and sinking into it, in rhythm with the horse's movement at a trot.

REINS: Narrow leather straps connecting the bridle with the rider's hands.

ROAN: A coat of any color evenly mixed with white.

SADDLE: Seat for a rider on a horse's back.

SADDLE HORN: The projection on the pommel of a western saddle, originally used to hold the lariat.

SEAT: The position of the rider in the saddle. The term refers to the entire body, not just the part in contact with the saddle.

SNAFFLE: A bit which is jointed in the middle with large metal rings at each end. The reins are attached to the rings.

SNIP: A white mark at or between the horse's nostrils.

SORREL: A western term for the lighter shades of chestnut.

STALLION: An uncastrated male horse.

STAR: A patch of white on the horse's forehead.

STIRRUP: The support for the rider's foot.

STOCKING: The white leg of a horse.

TACK: The equipment used in riding: saddle, bridle, pad, martingale, girth, stirrups, etc.

TRACK: The riding path.

THROATLATCH: The part of the bridle passing under the horse's throat.

TROT: A gait where the horse's legs move in diagonal pairs.

WALK: A slow gait in which the feet are only slightly removed from the ground.

WITHERS: The ridge between the shoulder bones of a horse.

INDEX

academies, riding, 10, 17
Appaloosa, 12

bay, 11, 12
bight, 44
billets, 17, 24
bit, 19, 20, 25, 26, 31, 53
blaze, 13
blue roan, 12
boots, 28–29

breeches, 28, 29
bridle, 16, 19, 22, 25, 63

canter, 48, 58–60, 70, 72
cantle, 17, 33, 46
chaps, 28
cheekstraps, 63
chestnuts, 12
cinches, 17
coloring, 11–13

colt, 14
competition, 67, 71, 74
crop, 65–66
crownpiece, 19, 25, 26
curb bit, 20–22
curb chain, 21, 27
curb rein, 22, 44

derby, 29
diagonals, 55–57, 72
dismounting, 45–47, 66
double bridle, 22

England, 33
English riding boots, 28
English saddles, 17
English-style, 42
equipment, rider's, 27–30

figure eight, 71–72
filly, 14
flanks, 42
foreleg, 54, 57, 58, 59
France, 33
full bridle, 22

gaits, 48–49, 54, 62–64, 71. *See also* individual names
gallop, 48
gelding, 14
girth, 17, 22, 23, 24, 25, 33, 49, 55

hindleg, 54
hindquarters, 50

horsemanship, 68, 74
horse show, 67, 74
hunt boots, 28, 29

jodhpur boots, 28
jodhpur pants, 28, 29

lead, 31, 59, 71, 72
leading, 58
lessons, 10

mane, 33, 65
mare, 14
martingale, 22
mount, 23, 32, 33, 36, 37
mounting block, 36

neckreining, 50
noseband, 19, 22, 25

paces, 73
palomino, 12
pelham bit, 20–21
pinto, 12
pommel, 17, 35, 45
posting, 55–58

red roan, 12
reins, 19, 20, 21, 22, 25, 31, 32, 33, 37, 39, 42, 43, 44, 45, 49, 50, 52, 53, 55, 65, 66
reverse, 70
ribbons, 74
rider's equipment, 27–30

riding academies, 10, 17
roan, 12

saddle, 16, 17, 22, 23, 28, 33, 35, 36, 37, 38, 39, 42, 50, 52, 55, 56, 58, 59, 60
saddle flaps, 28
saddle pad, 18
saddle sores, 23
safety, 61–66
seat, 37–39, 41, 54
show, horse, 67, 74
show number, 69
skirts, 17
slack, 49, 55
snaffle bit, 20–22
snaffle rein, 22, 43, 44
snip, 14
sorrels, 12
stables, 10, 14
stallion, 14
star, 14
stirrup irons, 28, 33, 42
stirrup leathers, 17, 23, 28
stirrups, 17, 23, 33, 35, 36, 37, 38, 39, 41, 42, 46, 47, 55
stirrup treads. *See* treads
stocking, 14
strawberry roan, 12
stride, 56, 57, 72

tack, 16
"tack up," 23
three-finger grip, 42, 43, 44
throatlatch, 27
track, 62, 64
trail, 62, 63
tread, 41, 42
treats, 15
trot, 48, 54, 55, 56, 58, 70, 72
turning, 50–51

walk, 48–49, 51, 54, 55, 70, 72
Western saddles, 17
Western-style, 30, 45, 50
withers, 23, 33, 38, 39, 46